Labyrinth's Medley

Madhvi Shah

BookLeaf Publishing

Presentation by *BookLeaf Publishing*

Web: www.bookleafpub.com

E-mail: info@bookleafpub.com

ISBN: 978-93-95755-23-8

First edition 2022

Dedicated to -

- the best grandparents

- the most patient and kind mother

- the supportive soul sisters

- the cutest adoptive parents

a girl could ask for.

ACKNOWLEDGEMENT

I think of life as my favorite dish. It's a blend of sweet, sour, spicy, and bitter ingredients and I love it for all its flavors because my family is the secret ingredient that makes it all okay.

PREFACE

Always be brave, daring, and confident. - The motto of the Shah and Bhatt Family.

MY LOVE

For you my love I'm thankful for.
There are things I admire you for.

I admire your strength,
For it has strengthened me.
I admire your courage,
For it has heartened me.

I admire your passion,
For it has propelled me.
I admire your kindness,
For it has compelled me.

I admire your smart,
For it has enlightened me.
I admire your heart,
For it has delighted me.

MY FRIEND

All the sleepless nights will come to an end,
If you just believe in yourself, my friend.
Nights get tough when you let your head have its way,
But always remember there's a sunrise waiting for you the next day.

MIND & BODY

If you go through without strife,
You will thank yourself in the afterlife.

If you don't look at life in black and white,
You will always live your life quite right.

If you attempt to live life with control,
You will shy away from your goal.

If you reminisce about the horrid past,
Your time to relish now has passed.

SIMPLICITY OF LIFE

The beauty of life is as simple as breathing.
It's meant to be lived happily,
On the time that you're leasing.
You will find your way on the darkest path,
If you just reign on your own wrath.

HOW YOU LIVE

You think therefore you are.
You seek therefore you find.
You care therefore you feel.
You feel therefore you smile.

You see therefore you learn.
You learn therefore you change.
You change therefore you grow.
You grow therefore you gain.

You talk therefore you bond.
You bond therefore you love.
You live because you can.
You can because you're love.

You love therefore you trust.
You trust therefore you hold.
You hold for now and end.
For the end has just begun.

MY WONDER

I wonder what we live for.
I wonder who I need to survive for.
I wonder what we got time for.
I wonder who I'm right for.

I wonder what we fight for.
I wonder what I get the prize for.
I wonder who we turn on the light for.
I wonder who I need to smile for.

Looking in the mirror,

It's you who I live to write for.
It's you who I need to be alive for.

IN MY HEAD

I'm stronger than I think I am.
I keep myself away from the sham.
The sham of friendship,
That I secretly crave.
The sham of love-ship,
That I couldn't save.

CROSSING OVER

The quarrel amidst my mind and heart,
Is like day and night destined to stay apart.
Darkness one side,
Brightness another,
Becoming a lost soul further & further.

The restless clamoring of thoughts and plans,
Can't help a soul that won't trust their hands.
Be a thinker and a doer,
But live not with delusions of grandeur.

BE BRAVE

It takes courage to conceal emotion.
But more to get back to the love notion.
It seems easier to live life lonesome.
But you'll always rue that you couldn't show
some.
Courage is the word you're looking for.
Fleeing love? What for?

FOR YOU AND ME

Those one minute of exchanges,
Become ampleness for a lifetime.
Thought I could make changes,
But I've only been strong for the first time.

Have brainstormed all possibilities,
But this is the one that I crave.
To have you be called mine,
Is the only way for me to behave.

THE TUNE OF EVERY LOVE SONG

He got her a rose,
Like she was the one.
With one look they froze,
Their hearts came undone.

Their souls embrace,
But bodies stay afar.
Love becomes a maze,
Trust is their guiding star.

THE PEN IS MIGHTIER THAN THE SWORD

Every now and then,
Be fearless they say.
When I hold my pen,
It's limitless I'll say.

To be or not to be?
Is the question that plays.
Round and round three
Or four times a day.

The stories, the enchantment,
The forks in the way.
The cosmic feel of disbandment,
And a universe where I'm A-OK.

BELIEVE

Never say no, always say yes!
Improvise your way to inevitable success.
Not with finesse,
But with this mighty gift you possess.

Don’t let doubts & stress,
In the way of your progress.
Just say yes and I confess,
It won’t be yourself you’ll suppress.

THE ART OF FAITH

When your heart feels lost,
When your soul gains a friend.
When all obstacles are crossed,
When all is good in the end.

When your luck feels wrong,
When your day goes right.
When the pain gets strong,
When the heart feels all right.

When you have your faith,
You have mighty power,
To live not like a wraith,
But a gracious flower.

ONCE UPON A TIME

Once upon a time,
Life was a happy high.
Once upon a crime,
Life began to dissatisfy.

Once upon a trial,
Life was a labyrinth.
Once upon a denial,
Life appeared in length.

Once upon a confinement,
Life became a pique.
Once upon an assignment,
Life finds to seek.

A pleasure, a goal,
A happy high that,
Once used to be.
A love, a soul,
A meaningful act,
That is soon to be.

SAANS

We run and run and run off course,
When we trust we remain on course.
We fight and fight and fight to survive,
But only live when we come alive.

We pray and pray and pray for forgiveness
But get it only to our own address.
We love and love and love for delight,
But only feel it when we breathe in the light.

THERE'S A THREAD CONNECTED

There is a link that I have learned to share,
One with fear.
For there is no greater teacher than a scare.

There is a link that I always embrace,
One with happiness.
For there is euphoria I don't want to displace.

There is a link that I try not to treasure,
One with disgust.
For it is a reflex caused by displeasure.

There is a link that I pray will be brief,
One with despair.
For it's a hack that gets me through grief.

There is a link that I always embrace,
One with happiness.
For there is euphoria I don't want to displace.

There is a link that is my unwelcomed aggressor,
One with anger.
For it is a war lost to my worst possessor.

There is a link with all the amazing highs,
One with impulse.
For it is the world I want to surprise.

LIFE ALWAYS FINDS BALANCE

There is not one without the other.
For light is darkness' half-brother.

There is not one without the other.
For there are also despisers,
When there are lovers.

There is not one without the other.
A new life without a mother.

FAITH AND VERITY

People mistake it for possession,
For it is something you feel.
Some clutch to it for ascension,
Others fear it and kneel.

People sequester it in sorrow,
For it is not to be exploited.
Some bargain today and tomorrow,
But they're just the walking dead.

People look for the verity,
But find none.
Instead, look for clarity,
And find faith in someone.

THE LADY

Once upon a time,
She opened to the wrong pack.
But now in her prime.
Every bond is a flashback.

Mistakes have been her guru,
Yet she still fears to make another.
If only she just knew,
That life has promised her,
Blunders one after the other.

For that's how a girl's life should be,
To learn from her mistakes,
And not look up to a wannabe.
Because it's her life on stakes,
And she can be anything she wants to be.

THE END IS PART OF THE JOURNEY

Everything has a beginning middle and end,
And how it all goes isn't always penned.
The thought of peace is all we try to defend,
Every single day and even on the weekend.

Every single day, hour, minute, and second,
Makes us think and makes us contend.
The thought of who or what we intend,
To fight and love all the way to the year-end.

Childhood and adulthood make us overspend,
When old age comes, luck makes it a godsend.
We focus so much on how to get to the end,
We ignore our possibility to finally transcend.

www.ingramcontent.com/pod-product-compliance
Lightning Source LLC
Chambersburg PA
CBHW051758130826
49812CB00033B/1189
* 9 7 8 9 3 9 5 7 5 5 2 3 8 *